ULTIMATE SUPER MARIO RUN HANDBOOK

WRITTEN BY CHRIS SCULLION

CARLTON BOOKS

CONTENTS

WORLD 4

WORLD 5

WORLD 6

EXTRAS

INTRODUCTION

Welcome to the app-solutely amazing Super Mario Run! Although Mario has been a video game hero for more than 35 years, this is the first time ever that Nintendo's busy little plumber has appeared in a mobile game.

Super Mario Run is slightly different from the other games in the Super Mario Bros series. In previous games, you have full control over the direction and speed Mario runs, but in this game he's always running forward at full speed. This means you're going to have to think on your feet!

Whether you're completely new to Mario games or you've played them before, this handbook will tell you everything you need to know about Super Mario Run.

We'll take you through all 24 levels of the World Tour mode, then teach you how to master the expert Toad Rally mode and use it to unlock new decorations and buildings in the game's Kingdom Builder.

By the time we're done, you'll be a Super Mario Run master. So, without further ado...

LET'S-A GO!

1981
DONKEY KONG

Mario was created by Japanese designer, Shigeru Miyamoto. He first appeared in Donkey Kong as Jumpman. In this

game he had to climb to the top of a building to rescue his girlfriend, Pauline, from a giant ape. Donkey Kong was a massive hit.

1985
SUPER MARIO BROS

This is probably one of the most popular early Mario games. In it, Mario tries to rescue Princess Toadstool (later renamed Peach) from the evil King Koopa (now known as Bowser). It sold over 40 million copies and more than 30 years later, many Mario fans still think this is one of the best games ever made.

1983
MARIO BROS

Mario was so popular that Nintendo gave him his own game. Mario Bros was set in a sewer, full of enemies that you had to defeat. This

★ MARIO BROS., BATTLE THE PESTS! TWO PLAYERS MAKE IT EASIER.

game also introduced a brand new character: Mario's brother. Luigi looked just like Mario but he wore different coloured overalls!

1988
SUPER MARIO BROS 2

When it launched in Japan, Super Mario Bros 2 looked and played like Super Mario Bros, but it was much more difficult. Nintendo decided it would be too hard for the US and Europe, so a new and easier Super Mario Bros 2 was created.

1988 SUPER MARIO BROS 3

Although the first Super Mario Bros was the game that gave Mario his big break, it was the third game that made him a global superstar. For the first time ever, Mario could fly and he was able to wear suits that transformed him into a frog and even a Hammer Brother. But not everyone got to enjoy this game straight away! Super Mario Bros 3 came out in Japan in 1988 but it was 1991 before Europe got it!

1990 SUPER MARIO WORLD

When Nintendo released its new SNES console, there was only one guy it had to make sure was there from the start. Mario's fourth big game was enormous, with a massive world map and loads of hidden levels. More importantly though, Super Mario World marked the first appearance of Mario's dino chum Yoshi, who quickly became a favourite among fans.

1989 SUPER MARIO LAND

At the end of the '80s, Nintendo released the Game Boy, a handheld system that transformed the world of gaming. The Game Boy launched with two amazing games: Tetris and Super Mario Land. Mario's first handheld adventure took him to Sarasaland, a new world where Princess Daisy was being held prisoner by an evil space alien called Tatanga.

1992 SUPER MARIO KART

In the early '90s, Nintendo was working on a go-kart racing game. The characters were just normal racers wearing overalls until someone at Nintendo decided to replace them with Mario and friends for a joke. It went down so well that Super Mario Kart was born. Since then, there have been eight Mario Kart games and the series has sold over 100 MILLION copies worldwide!

THE HISTORY OF MARIO

1996 SUPER MARIO 64

Nintendo's third console, the Nintendo 64, ran 3D games instead of 2D ones. This meant Mario had to go 3D, too. The result was Super Mario 64, which was so ground-breaking it ended up writing a lot of the rules for the 3D games that followed. Crash Bandicoot, Spyro, and Ratchet & Clank all owe a lot to Super Mario 64.

2000 PAPER MARIO

Mario games aren't always about running and jumping (or racing), you know. At the turn of the millennium, Nintendo brought out Paper Mario, a role-playing game (RPG) in which a flat Mario had to rescue seven Star Spirits from Bowser's minions. Since it was an RPG, Paper Mario had more of a story than other Mario games and it was a funny one. There have since been five Paper Mario games in total.

2002 SUPER MARIO SUNSHINE

Super Mario 64 was such a big hit that fans were desperate for a sequel, and when it arrived it was very different! Super Mario Sunshine was a GameCube game in which Mario carried a special water pump called FLUDD. A fake Mario had slopped paint all over a tropical island so it was up to Mario to clear his name by cleaning it all up.

2003 MARIO & LUIGI: SUPERSTAR SAGA

In 2003, Nintendo handed the keys to Mario over to another Japanese company called AlphaDream. It came up with Mario & Luigi: Superstar Saga. In this RPG, Mario and Luigi have to fight a witch called Cackletta after she steals Princess Peach's voice. Superstar Saga was such a success that AlphaDream made four more games in the Mario & Luigi series. The most recent was Mario & Luigi: Paper Jam on the 3DS.

2006
NEW SUPER MARIO BROS

Believe it or not, by 2006 there hadn't been a side-scrolling Mario game for 14 years! That all changed when Nintendo made New Super Mario Bros for the DS. This was a brand new adventure that took Mario back to his roots by having him run from left to right all over again. New Super Mario Bros sold over 30 million copies, and since then Nintendo has made sequels for the Wii, 3DS and Wii U.

2007
SUPER MARIO GALAXY

When the Wii came out in 2006, its Mario game wasn't ready. Super Mario Galaxy launched a year later and fans quickly agreed it was one of the best games ever made. Putting Mario in space meant Nintendo could create all sorts of weird and wonderful lands with gravity-defying stunts, combined with a soundtrack performed by a real orchestra!

2015
SUPER MARIO MAKER

Nintendo's been coming up with Mario games for over 30 years, but have you ever had a brilliant Mario-inspired idea? That was the thinking behind Super Mario Maker. This was a Wii and 3DS game that let you create your own Mario levels to share online for others to play. By May 2016, more than 7 million levels had been uploaded – that's a lot of Mario to play through!

2016
SUPER MARIO RUN

For some time now, fans have wanted to see Mario on their mobile phones, and in 2016 Nintendo finally agreed. Super Mario Run is an app that... hey, you already know what it is. Why else would you have this book? What you really want to know is how to master it, don't you? Well, read on and we'll tell you everything you need to know!

WORLD TOUR MODE

World Tour mode is the first of Super Mario Run's three modes. It's also the one that's most like previous Mario games because you run, jump and bounce your way through its 24 levels to rescue Princess Peach.

Even if you're a Mario expert, there are still plenty of tricks and traps to keep you on your toes. The coloured coin challenges test even the best Mario players.

But if you're completely new to Mario, never fear! We've broken down every single level so you know exactly which enemies and obstacles to expect and how to deal with them. Good luck!

SIX OF THE BEST

There are six worlds, each with four levels, in World Tour mode. In fine Mario tradition, the fourth level in each world is either a fortress or an airship, with a boss to greet you at the end. Beat the boss to unlock the next world and win tickets for Toad Rally mode (see page 62). The first time you complete all four levels in a world, you unlock the same levels in Toad Rally.

COINING IT IN

If you reckon you've mastered all 24 levels, try the coloured coin challenges. Each level has five pink coins hidden away in it. Get them all in one run and you'll get some Toad Rally tickets. The next time you play the level, there'll be five purple coins hidden in even harder to find locations. After you've found these, five even trickier black coins will be waiting for you. Can you find every pink, purple and black coin in the game?

CHOOSE WISELY!

Although you start with Mario, you'll eventually unlock other characters to play in the game. When you choose a level, you'll see a little picture of Mario in the bottom-right. Tap that before you start the level and you'll be able to change your character. See page 70 to find out how to unlock the other five characters.

1-1: UP AND OVER

Welcome to World Tour mode! The first level is an easy introduction to the world of Super Mario Run and lets you meet some of the most well-known Mario enemies in case you're new to the series.

PAUSE BLOCKS

These red Pause Blocks are new to Mario. Even though Mario is always running in Super Mario Run (the clue's in the name!) there are times when he might need to stop. Run over a red Pause Block and Mario will stand still until you tap the screen. This lets you plan ahead and figure out which way to go next.

COIN ARROWS

Each level in Super Mario Run has arrows guiding you along the way. These arrows aren't just there to show you where to go though. Run over them and a row of coins will appear. Follow the arrows closely in each level and you'll end up with a tidy chunk of change.

GOOMBAS

It wouldn't be a Mario game without these little brown mushroom creatures. Even if you're new to Mario games, Goombas are easy to beat. Just jump on their heads and you'll squish them. Don't feel bad – they aren't very nice so they deserve to be taught a lesson!

TOP TIP!

Most levels in Super Mario Run finish when you reach the flagpole at the end. The trick is to hit the flagpole as high as you can to get the most coins – up to a maximum of 10. Sometimes you need to do a midair spin to reach the top (see World 1-4).

KOOPA TROOPAS

Where there are Goombas, you know Koopa Troopas can't be far behind. You can jump on them, too! This makes them go into their shells, which you can kick at other enemies. In Super Mario Run, the shell is kicked automatically as soon as you hit it.

1-2: WALL-KICKING IT UNDERGROUND

It's Mario tradition for the second level to always be an underground stage and Super Mario Run is no different. This level is where you'll get to try wall-jumping for the first time.

PIRANHA PLANTS

These nasty chompers can take a bite out of you if you're not careful – mainly because you can't jump on their heads like you can other enemies. If you stand next to their pipe, they won't come out. So, don't be afraid to run into the side of the pipe, stop and take your time to avoid being hurt.

⭐ TOP TIP!

In Super Mario Run, if Mario runs into a bad guy, he does a cool little hurdle over them. Tap the screen while Mario's hurdling and he'll somersault off them, which is really useful in Toad Rally mode.

SLOPE-SLIDING

When Mario goes down a steep slope, he'll ride down it on his backside. When he's like this, he can bash through any enemies on the slope with the greatest of ease. Most of the slopes in this game let you reach special higher areas if you jump off them early, so keep your eyes peeled.

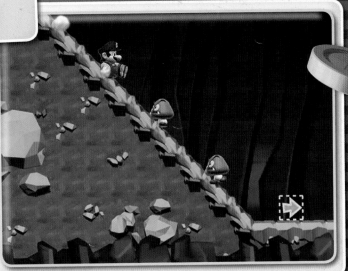

WALL-JUMPS

Wall-jumping is one of the most important skills in Super Mario Run because it can help you reach higher areas, and can save you if a jump goes wrong. Jump into a wall and Mario will start sliding down it. All you have to do is tap the screen and he'll jump off the wall in the opposite direction. If you can find two walls facing each other, keep doing this to climb them.

SPRINGBOARDS

These big yellow springboards chuck Mario much higher than you might expect. They only spring when you tap the screen but be careful because they launch you straight up. Only tap when you're right underneath the coins or blocks you want to hit.

17

1-3: PARATROOPAS IN MUSHROOM VALLEY

The third level takes place on loads of giant mushrooms – hope you aren't afraid of heights! This is where you'll find a new enemy, the Koopa Paratroopa.

KOOPA PARATROOPAS

OK, they're just Koopa Troopas with wings, but being able to fly makes Koopa Paratroopas a bit more dangerous. Because they're slightly taller than Koopa Troopas, you can't flip over them and if you hit them from the side you'll get hurt. This means the only way you can beat a Paratroopa is by jumping on its head. You can reach special coins or items high above Paratroopas by bouncing off them. So, pay attention to what's above each Paratroopa as you get near it.

SPEED BLOCKS

World 1-3 is the first time you'll come across these special yellow blocks with arrows on them. Run over them and you won't go any faster, but jump when you're on one and you'll do an Olympian long jump! It's a fast jump though, so make sure you're ready for whatever is waiting for you when you land because you won't have much time to react to it.

RED RINGS

These red rings give you a mini-game when you run through them. Five red coins will appear and you only have a few seconds to get them all. Pull it off and you'll get a Star, which will let you gather loads of coins and kill any enemy. Don't pull it off and... well, you won't. Red ring mini-games take a bit of practice because all of the coins have to be collected in one go. If you miss a coin, you won't have enough time to go back and get it before it disappears.

DIAGONAL BLOCKS

Diagonal Blocks are like your normal red Pause Blocks, but with a twist. Instead of moving you forward when you tap the screen, they make you jump. This means they're useful for when you want to stop and time a tricky jump. But sometimes it's dangerous to take the high road so use these Diagonal Blocks with care.

TOP TIP!

Bounce off a Paratroopa and its shell springs forward, zapping all in its path!

1-4: BOWSER'S CASTLE HANGOUT

Here we go! It's already time to meet Bowser! Well, sort of. He may look like Mario's sworn enemy but something about him just doesn't seem right...

DRY BONES

Bowser's castle levels always have these creepy skeleton versions of Koopa Troopas. Jumping on Dry Bones crumbles them into a pile of bones, but soon they form back together again. While this can be a problem in other Mario games, here Mario's usually long gone before a Dry Bones can pull itself together, so treat them like normal enemies!

TOP TIP!

Any time Mario's in the air (whether he's jumping or falling), you can make him do a little spin by tapping the screen. This isn't just there to look cool, though. When Mario spins he stays in the air a little longer and moves more to the side. This allows you to make bigger jumps and land on enemies further away.

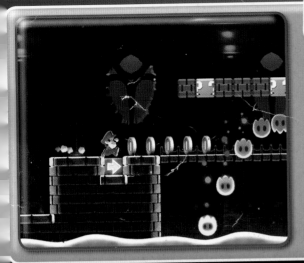

LAVA BUBBLES

While Dry Bones are easier to deal with here, Lava Bubbles are the opposite. These jump out of the lava and, if you can't avoid them, you take damage. And in Super Mario Run, sometimes it's impossible to avoid them. Thankfully, most Lava Bubbles have stop blocks just before them. If you stand on stop blocks and wait for the right time to tap the screen, you can run past them.

BOSS LEVEL

Wow! This game must be easy if you get the chance to beat Bowser so early on, right? Actually, it isn't really Bowser but a Goomba in disguise. The aim is to hit the axe that's behind him and send him into the lava. (Time it right when you hit the axe and you'll reveal the sneaky Goomba under the Bowser disguise.) If you've eaten a mushroom and are big, you can run through this fake Bowzer to send him into the lava. Otherwise you'll need to get past him. The easiest way is to stand on the stop block and wait for him to jump. As soon as he lands, you should start running, jump over him and do a midair spin to make sure you jump clear without touching him.

2-1: GHOST-DOOR DECEPTION

It's time for Super Mario Run's first Ghost House! These ghosts play tricks on you to try to confuse you and get you lost. Since you don't have a big time limit, you don't want that to happen!

STRETCHES

A Stretch is a special kind of Boo who lies on a floor or roof, and pops out every now and then. Just like Boos, you can't hurt a Stretch so the best thing to do is stay away from them. Sometimes you need to get past them to get through the level or hit a power-up block. Make sure you time this well so you get to them when they're lying down. Even though they're right there, as long as you don't see them, they won't hurt you.

GREEN DOORS

This level is made up of a bunch of different rooms, each with three green doors. Only one door is real and takes you to the next room, the rest take you back to the start of the room you're already in. Take your time and keep your eye on each of the doors. Two of them will shake every now and then. The real door is the one that doesn't shake. Don't try to memorise which one it is because it's a different door every time you play the level.

BOOS

These ghosts are really shy. When Mario looks in their direction, they stop and hide, but when he turns away, they chase after him. That doesn't really affect you in Super Mario Run because you're only going in one direction, but you should still be careful if you see a Boo because you can't hurt them. Whether they're hiding or not, you'll take damage as soon as you touch one.

TIME BLOCKS

Ghost House levels are full of tricks designed to get you lost so if you can't figure them out quickly, you might end up running out of time. Luckily, in each Ghost House these special purple time blocks are here to help with that. Hit one and you'll get some extra time added to the clock, making it easier for you to reach the end without all your lovely seconds disappearing.

2-2: SKY-HIGH LIFTS AND LEAPS!

Mario takes to the skies in this level and uses midair lifts to get around. Hope you don't have a fear of heights because you'll need to do some death-defying jumps to beat this level!

AIR LIFTS

A big chunk of this level is made up of these yellow lifts. They don't move at first but as soon as you land on one it will start following the track it's attached to. Mario won't run when he's standing on a platform, and will only jump off when you tap the screen, so take your time and don't jump until you're completely ready. You don't often get a chance to slow things down in this game, so make the most of it!

⭐ TOP TIP!

Bounce high off an enemy and if you land on another, you'll get extra coins. With practice, you can bounce on five or more enemies without touching the ground and get loads of coins. Use the midair spin to help you aim your bounces.

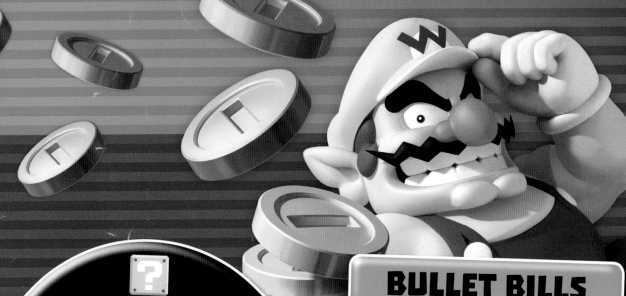

? FACT!

Bullet Bill may be an odd name for a big missile with a face on it, but it makes them sound quite friendly. That isn't the case in Japan, where they aren't called Bullet Bills. Instead, they're called Killers. Steady on!

BULLET BILLS

Everything has a personality in a Mario game, even missiles. These large bullets can come at you from either direction, but they move quite slowly so you don't have to worry about them too much. You might imagine bullets would hurt you but you can bounce off a Bullet Bill as if it were a normal enemy. It's just a bit harder to line up your jump because although they're slow, they still move faster than Goombas or Koopa Troopas.

P-SWITCHES

These blue switches appear in a bunch of Mario games and do all sorts of things. In Super Mario Run, they usually have one job. If you jump on them, they'll make blue coins appear for a few seconds. This may not be such a big deal in World Tour mode but in Toad Rally mode, where every coin counts, they're really important.

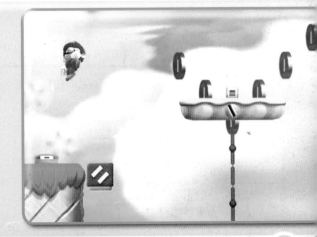

2-3: TREASURE-HOARDING SWOOPS

For some reason Mario just can't get enough of going underground, and level 2-3 has him heading back down there. This time you'll face off against nasty bat creatures called Swoops.

SWOOPS

These bats hang from the ceiling until Mario approaches them. Then they'll swoop down (yes, that's why they're called that) and fly in a straight line towards him. This makes them quite easy to jump onto. So, unless you're in a narrow corridor and don't have a lot of jumping space above you, Swoops aren't too tricky to beat.

STEP BOUNCING

Sometimes Mario games send a group of enemies at you in a certain way to help you reach a hidden area. This happens in this level, when a bunch of Swoops come at you from different heights. If you bounce off each of them one at a time, as if they were a set of steps, you'll get higher and higher until you reach a pink coin at the top.

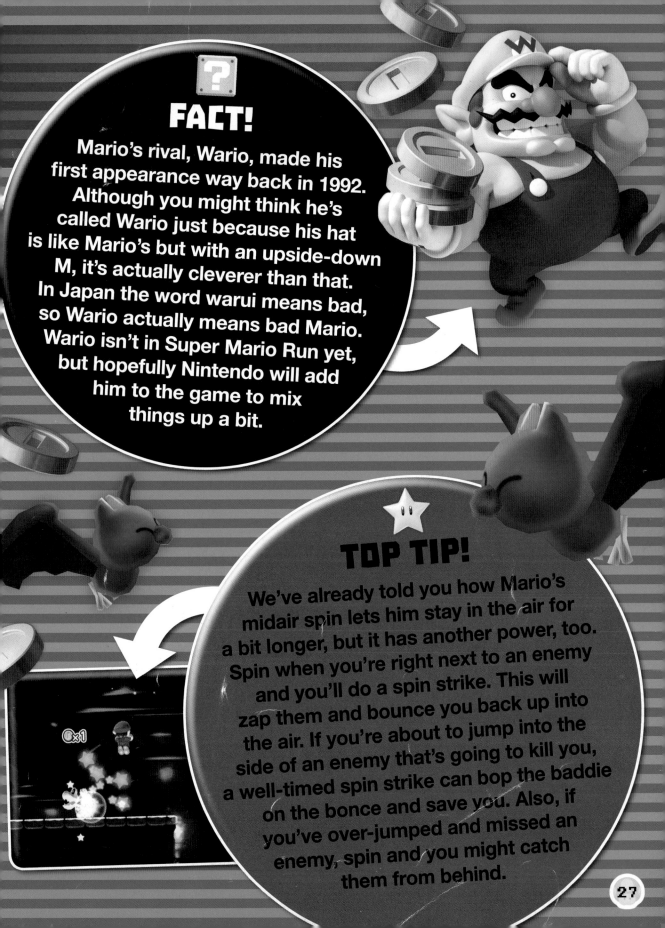

FACT!

Mario's rival, Wario, made his first appearance way back in 1992. Although you might think he's called Wario just because his hat is like Mario's but with an upside-down M, it's actually cleverer than that. In Japan the word warui means bad, so Wario actually means bad Mario. Wario isn't in Super Mario Run yet, but hopefully Nintendo will add him to the game to mix things up a bit.

TOP TIP!

We've already told you how Mario's midair spin lets him stay in the air for a bit longer, but it has another power, too. Spin when you're right next to an enemy and you'll do a spin strike. This will zap them and bounce you back up into the air. If you're about to jump into the side of an enemy that's going to kill you, a well-timed spin strike can bop the baddie on the bonce and save you. Also, if you've over-jumped and missed an enemy, spin and you might catch them from behind.

2-4: AIRSHIP CANNONS... FIRE!

Now you're in trouble! This is the first of three airship levels in the game. One false step here will send you plummeting to your doom. On top of this, if you make it to the end, you'll have the nasty Boom Boom to deal with.

CANNONBALLS

Bowser's airships are basically big pirate ships that can fly, and you can't have a pirate ship without cannons. These ones fire cannonballs up at an angle which means you can't hurdle them – you take a hit instead. If you're skillful enough, however, you can jump onto them and bounce off to safety. So, there's no need to completely dodge them.

? FACT!

Bowser's first airship appeared back in 1988 in Super Mario Bros 3 and there have been lots more since then. In New Super Mario Bros U, each of Bowser's seven kids has their own special airship with their face on it! Bowser must have more money than sense.

NINJIS

You might not know Ninjis that well, even though they've been appearing in Mario games for nearly 30 years. They're tricky little fellas! They jump up and down on the spot so if you time your jump wrong, you clatter into them and take a hit. Luckily Mario can jump higher than a Ninji so if you're on the same level you should be able to jump over them no problem. Sometimes though, they're standing on taller platforms, which means you have to wait until they drop to the ground before you can jump over them.

BOSS LEVEL

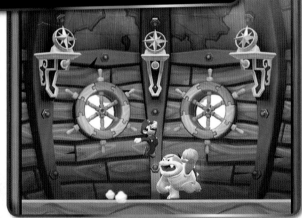

Boom Boom is one of Bowser's most loyal henchmen, and he often steps up to battle Mario when Bowser isn't ready to face him. He can be a pretty scary-looking guy if you don't know how to tackle him, but once you do, he's quite easy to beat. You have to jump on his head three times to win. The best way to do this is to jump on it once, then run over to a wall and stand next to it. When Boom Boom runs at you, jump into the wall and Mario will slide down it, as if he's getting ready to do a wall-jump. Slide right down onto Boom Boom's head and you'll bounce off him. When you land, run to the other wall, repeat and Boom Boom will meet his doom!

3-1: BIG SPINY BLITZ

So far you've probably been happy hopping from platform to platform, bouncing on baddies' heads. That's all about to change. It's time to meet the Big Spiny, and you definitely don't want to bounce on him!

YELLOW '!' SWITCHES

In some levels, you'll come across yellow switches with a big exclamation mark on them. They're usually placed near invisible red blocks with dotted outlines showing where they are. Step on the switch and you'll make these blocks appear, but be careful because you'll also turn any normal red blocks invisible.

BIG SPINIES

Spinies are one of the most common Mario enemies, but in Super Mario Run you'll come across this special supersize version first. It should be pretty obvious, but Mario's usual trick of jumping onto enemies won't work here! Dodge them instead, unless you end up finding a Star to give you invincibility.

LAKITU

This little Koopa chap flies around in a cloud and can never decide whether to be a good guy or a bad guy. In this level, you're in luck because he's on your side. At first he'll be carrying one of the level's five coloured coins, and once you nab that he'll start throwing normal coins at you. It's good when he's nice like this, but enjoy it while it lasts because in a few levels' time, he'll be in a bad mood.

FACT!

Lakitu has had tons of different Mario-related jobs over the years. In Mario Kart, he fishes your kart out every time you fall into water or down a hole. He was most useful in Super Mario 64 though, where he played the cameraman following Mario around so you could play the game. In one area, you could see his reflection in the mirror!

3-2: BULLET BILL BARRAGE

Bullet Bills are back, and this time they've brought their angrier cousins. You'll need to stay on your toes to make sure you don't get bopped by a Bull's-Eye Bill!

BULL'S-EYE BILLS

A Bull's-Eye Bill is a much angrier version of a Bullet Bill, which is why it's red instead of black. They'll come from behind you at a normal speed but when they get close, they'll suddenly go quicker. You can still jump on them like you can with Bullet Bills, but because they change speed you need to be more careful and make sure you time it right.

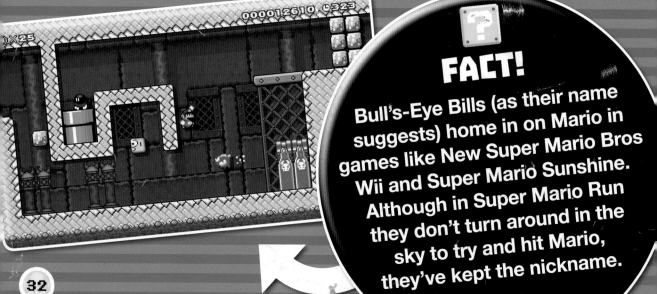

FACT!

Bull's-Eye Bills (as their name suggests) home in on Mario in games like New Super Mario Bros Wii and Super Mario Sunshine. Although in Super Mario Run they don't turn around in the sky to try and hit Mario, they've kept the nickname.

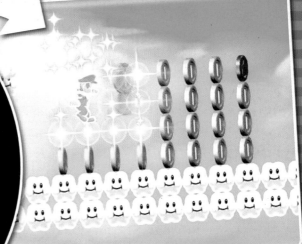

FACT!

There have been nearly 20 different types of Bullet Bill over the years! There's an underwater version (Torpedo Ted), a cat-like Super Mario 3D World version, and a massive one called Banzai Bill who's featured in a bunch of Mario games. You can identify Banzai Bill by his big teeth.

3-3: SHELL ME THE WAY!

Kicking a shell is one of the most fun things you can do in a Mario game, so here's an entire level built around doing just that. Time to get your booting boots on!

KICKING A SHELL

You'll already have jumped on Koopa Troopas and kicked their shells by this point, but this is the first level that shows you just how useful it can be. Hit a shell and follow it for as long as you can and it will plough through loads of enemies, giving you lots of coins every time. Levels like this are a great way to gather coins if you need them for Kingdom Builder mode.

MUNCHERS

These little lads look like baby Piranha Plants, but they're actually one of the toughest enemies in the game because you can't kill them. Even with a Star, you can only run over the top of them. The best thing you can do is to just avoid them, but do bear in mind that you can still kick shells onto them and they'll skim along the top.

FACT!

Ever wondered what a Koopa Troopa wears under his shell? Some Mario games have answered this question for you. If you jump on one in Super Mario World or Super Mario 3D World, the poor Koopa Troopa will pop out of his shell, leaving him standing there in his little white vest. Well, at least he keeps it clean!

TOP TIP!

An expert trick in this level lets you ride kicked shells. Make Mario do a fast long jump using a speed arrow. Time it right and you'll land on top of the shell and keep bouncing on it, beating enemies and winning coins as you go.

3-4: FIRE BAR CASTLE! YOUCH!

After beating the fake Bowser at the end of World 1, another Bowser has taken its place. Something about this one doesn't look quite right either though... could this one be a fake, too?

FIRE BARS

Fire bars appeared in the very first Bowser level in the first ever Super Mario Bros game in 1985… and they're back! They're made entirely of fire so you can't damage them. Instead you have to make sure you get past them with a well-timed run. You can also jump over them if you need to, and if you have a Star, you can pass right through them.

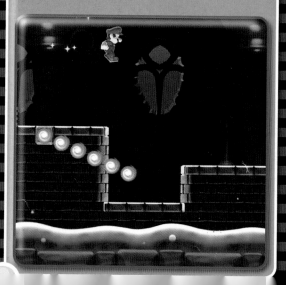

★ TOP TIP!

Killing Mario makes him return in a bubble which floats backwards until you pop it. If you've missed some coloured coins, kill him, follow him back to where you took the wrong path, pop the bubble and try again. Caution: you can only do this twice!

FACT!

Mario's fiercest foe has always been the evil Bowser, but he didn't always go by that name. In the first ever Super Mario Bros game, he was known as King Koopa. In Japan, where the Mario games come from, he's still called Koopa to this day. That's where Koopa Troopas got their name: they're troopers that fight for Koopa!

BOSS LEVEL

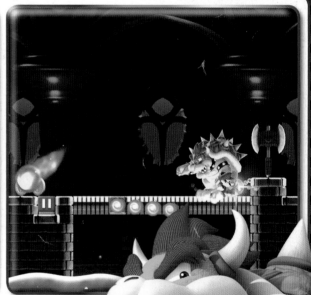

So, is this the real Bowser? Afraid not! It's a camouflaged Koopa Troopa. The trick to beating him is to reach the axe and send him tumbling into the lava below. Be careful, though, because there's a big fire bar in the way and this fake Bowser spits a fireball at you when he jumps. Stand on the pause block and be patient. Eventually you'll find the right time to run at him and jump over him to reach the axe. If you have a Mushroom, you can reach the axe much more easily by running straight through him and taking a hit.

4-1: CUTTING-EDGE SPIRE

Most levels in Mario games have you running from left to right, but sometimes it's good to brush up on your wall-climbing skills and start going up in the world instead.

GOING UP!

If you aren't good at wall-jumping, you might struggle in this level because this is what you'll be doing more than anything else. Take your time and don't try to rush wall-jumps. We know it can be tempting to try to do them quickly but, if you time one badly, you could end up falling way back down to the bottom of the section you're on – and that can waste a lot more time!

GRINDERS

You don't need us to tell you that these spinning blades are bad news. Get near one and it will hurt you quicker than you can say, "Hmm, that looks a bit sharp." Some blades don't move but be extra careful of the ones that slide along rails. Some of these move quite fast so make sure you leave yourself enough space to get past them safely.

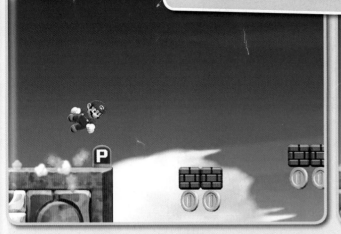

P switches aren't just useful for turning blocks into coins, they also work the opposite way. If you can see a hard-to-reach area with some coins below it, hit the P switch and you'll turn the coins into blocks you can jump on to get higher. So if you see coins above a P switch, don't collect them because they might be more useful to you as a platform a few seconds later.

FACT!

Did you know that Mario may have actually been wearing the wrong coloured overalls for 25 years? In Donkey Kong and the first two Super Mario Bros games, he wore red overalls with a blue shirt. When Super Mario Bros 3 came out, the colours had switched and they've been like that ever since. Did his local clothes shop run out of red overalls, or has he just been wearing his spare pair all these years? We'll never know!

4-2: SLOPE TO SUCCESS

You've already slid down a few slopes by this point, but here's your chance to show whether you've mastered it. This level will have you spending more time on your backside than your feet!

SLOPE TO SLOPE

A couple of sections of this level have been designed to get Mario sliding for ages. When you get to the bottom of a slope, you can jump off and land right on the next slope if you time it right. This doesn't just look cool, it keeps your enemy combo going. Sliding into lines of Goombas or Koopa Troopas gets you one, then two, then four coins. But if you jump from one slope to another straight into a slide, you'll keep getting the maximum four coins instead of going back to one again.

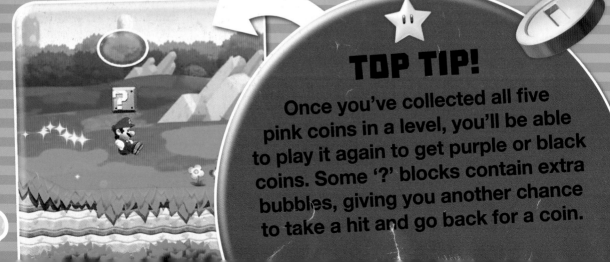

TOP TIP!

Once you've collected all five pink coins in a level, you'll be able to play it again to get purple or black coins. Some '?' blocks contain extra bubbles, giving you another chance to take a hit and go back for a coin.

CANNONS

These cannons aren't like the cannons from the airship level – these ones are here to help you. Jump into a cannon and it will start moving slowly. Time it right and tap when you're at just the right angle to collect the coins. Don't be annoyed if you don't succeed at first because it can be really difficult to get the timing right. The more you play this level, the more skilled you'll become and the easier cannon control will be.

FACT!

Bubbles might feel like a new feature in Mario games, but they've actually helped protect Mario for a long time... ever since he was a baby, in fact! In Yoshi's Island, Yoshi had to carry Baby Mario on his back through each level. Any time you took a hit, Baby Mario would get knocked into the sky and float around in a bubble, protecting him from enemies, until Yoshi could pop it and get him back. Just think, if there had been no bubbles, Mario might never have grown up into the hero he is today!

4-3: DANGER HIGH AND LOW

You won't find many safe spots in this level! With Munchers below and Piranha Plants above, you'll have enough on your plate without having to deal with a brand new enemy as well.

BUZZY BEETLES

Unlike Goombas, these little beasties have hard shells, which means you can't squash them. You can, however, jump onto them and kick their shells, just like you can Koopa Troopas. In other Mario games, they are exactly the same as Koopa Troopas, except you can't kill them with fireballs. Since there are no fireballs in this game, there's no difference at all, so treat them in exactly the same way as you would Koopa Troopas.

SPINNING BUZZY BEETLES

Some Buzzy Beetles crawl on the ceiling and then drop down and start spinning towards you. These can be trickier to deal with than normal Buzzy Beetles. You can't run right into them or hurdle them – you'll get hurt. You have to either jump over them or, if you time it right, jump onto them and send them spinning off in the other direction. Make sure they don't hit a wall and come back though!

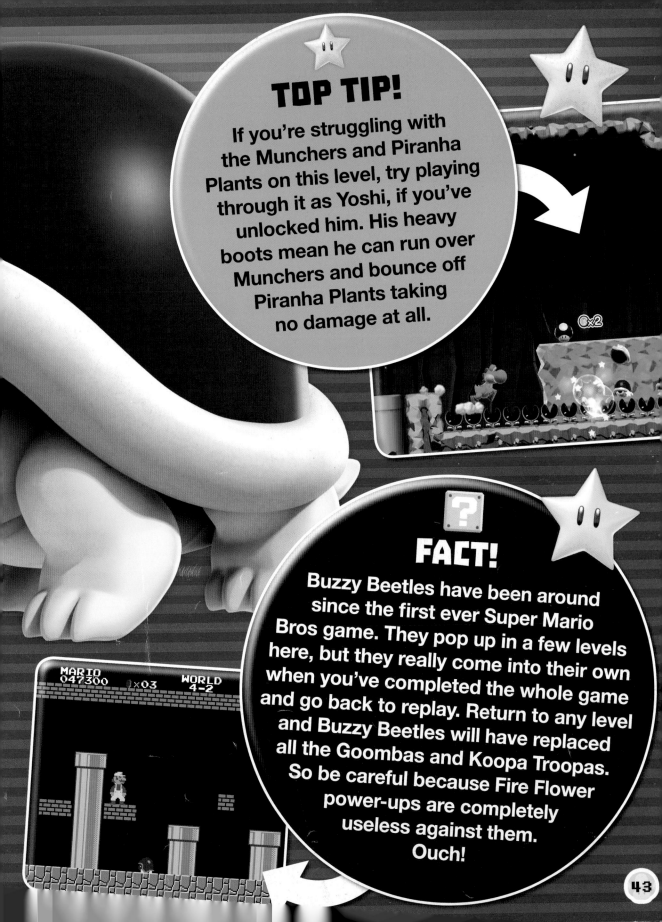

TOP TIP!

If you're struggling with the Munchers and Piranha Plants on this level, try playing through it as Yoshi, if you've unlocked him. His heavy boots mean he can run over Munchers and bounce off Piranha Plants taking no damage at all.

FACT!

Buzzy Beetles have been around since the first ever Super Mario Bros game. They pop up in a few levels here, but they really come into their own when you've completed the whole game and go back to replay. Return to any level and Buzzy Beetles will have replaced all the Goombas and Koopa Troopas. So be careful because Fire Flower power-ups are completely useless against them. Ouch!

MARIO 047300 ×03 WORLD 4-2

4-4: FIRING THE AIRSHIP'S BURNERS

Boom Boom's back, and he's brought a new airship with him. We hope you don't mind things heating up because in this level there are loads of Burners shooting flames at you from every direction.

BURNERS

The new and improved airship has a bunch of these hot obstacles placed all over it. As soon as you see small flickers of fire coming out of them, get out of the way because this means they're about to shoot out massive jets of flame. If you haven't seen Burners in other Mario games before, it might take a while to get used to them. Once you get the timing right, these should be easy to avoid though.

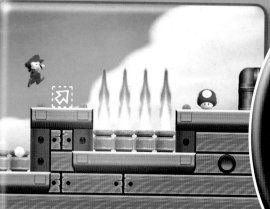

? FACT!

Believe it or not, Boom Boom actually has a girlfriend. Pom Pom appears in some boss fights in Super Mario 3D Land for Nintendo 3DS, brandishing a boomerang with a pink ribbon on it. Imagine the damage at their wedding, if they ever got married!

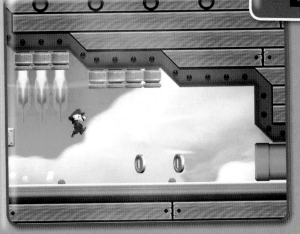

BIGGER IS BETTER

Most boss levels can be tricky because there's a good chance you might take a hit while fighting them. The game knows this and does its best to help you. So, keep your eyes peeled as you approach a boss because there's almost always a Super Mushroom nearby. Grab it and you'll be able to take one hit without dying and having to start all over again.

BOSS LEVEL

You can't keep Boom Boom down! Even though you beat him in World 2, he's back to settle the score. As in World 2-4, you can beat Boom Boom by jumping on his head three times. However, the same wall-sliding method won't work this time because there are Burners under each wall which will hurt you if you slide all the way down. Instead, start to slide down the wall and then do a wall jump as Boom Boom runs over to you. If you time it right, you'll land on his head. If you miss, you'll jump over him and you can run over to the other wall and try it again. Keep trying until you hit him three times and boom! Boom Boom's finished.

5-1: LAKITU'S REVENGE

He may have been nice a few levels ago, but Lakitu's had one of his typical mood swings and now he's gunning for you. Can you outrun his Spiny assault?

LAKITU GOES BAD

Back in World 3-1, Lakitu was chucking coins at you, but now he's slinging Spinies, too. Sometimes he'll throw a Spiny, other times he'll throw a coin. By the time you've seen what he's thrown, it's usually too late to decide whether to collect it or avoid it. The best strategy is to steer clear of him completely. After all, you can get coins anywhere.

TOP TIP!

You can actually run through this whole level with invincibility! To do this, collect all the Super Stars hidden in the blocks on the top path. If you get a new one whilst you are still invincible from the last, you'll keep it going until you hit the final flagpole!

FACT!

Mario's creator, Shigeru Miyamoto, once said that Lakitu was the character that was most like him. Miyamoto explained that Lakitu, "seems to be very free, floating in the air, going anywhere," and that's something he likes the idea of. We hope he only sees himself as nice Lakitu. It's hard to imagine this creative genius destroying his characters with Spinies!

FUZZIES

If you touch these funny-looking enemies, it's no laughing matter! Unless you have a Super Star, there's no way to hurt them. Most of them move along rails, so keep well away from these, especially on sections where you're jumping across yellow platforms. Take your time and you should be fine.

5-2: POKEY VAULTING

Pokey's are 20-foot tall, waddling cactuses with smiley faces... and they are covered in super-sharp spikes! It's time to head to the desert to take them on...

POKEYS

A Pokey is a big cactus that hurts you if you touch it. They come in two forms: those that stand still and those that move slowly towards you. This means they're pretty easy to dodge if you're good at judging how high Mario can jump. Because most Pokeys are tall, you need to make sure Mario's right at the top of his jump when he passes over them so he can clear them without touching their spiky heads.

? FACT!

Pokeys cause Mario problems in lots of different games, except for one – Mario Pinball Land for Game Boy Advance. For some reason, when Mario is rolled into a ball and fired at a Pokey with a big flipper, it's the Pokey that ends up worse off. Don't try this the next time you see a cactus, though!

SHELL SHOCKED

In this level, you can use a few Koopa Troopa shells to bring the Pokeys down to size a bit. But be careful! If a Pokey is made up of only two segments, the shell will kill it. If it's made up of three or more segments, it will only remove one. If you're running behind a shell and it hits a Pokey made up of three segments, get ready to jump because he'll still be there once the shell's gone through him.

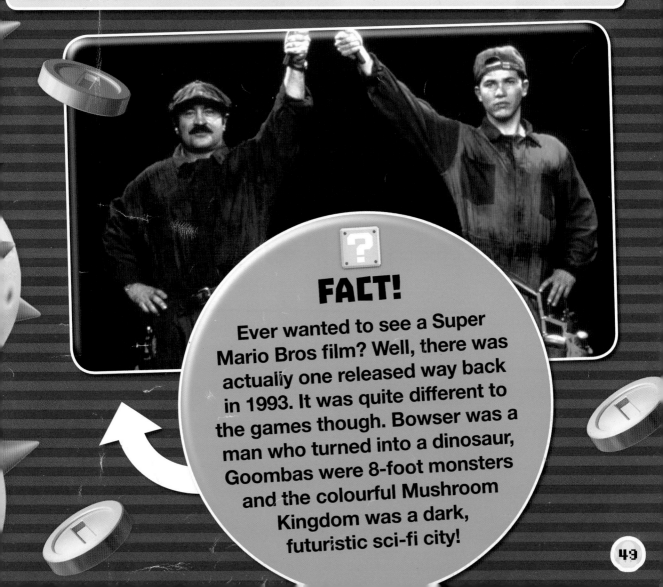

FACT!

Ever wanted to see a Super Mario Bros film? Well, there was actually one released way back in 1993. It was quite different to the games though. Bowser was a man who turned into a dinosaur, Goombas were 8-foot monsters and the colourful Mushroom Kingdom was a dark, futuristic sci-fi city!

5-3: BOOHIND LOCK AND KEY

We hope you're ready because you're about to tackle one of the hardest levels in the game. And why is it so tricky? Well, you are going to have to kill a Boo and that's no mean feat! Pay attention because there's a knack to this...

KEYS

Every Ghost House has a special gimmick and this one is no different. You have to make your way through a series of rooms by finding keys and opening locked doors. The first key is waiting for you at the top of the first room and the second key is hiding in blocks at the top of the next room – all easy enough. It's the third key that makes this an annoying level. Read on to find out more...

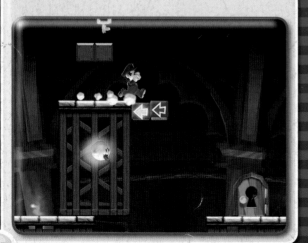

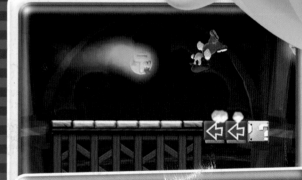

KILLING A BOO

The third and final key in this level is actually hidden inside a Boo in the third room. You can see the key inside it as it floats around but how do you get it out? Well, you have to kill the Boo and Mario can't kill a Boo just by jumping on its head. He has to do a backflip over it. So you'll need to jump onto the blue back arrows at the top of the room, then tap the screen to do a backflip and hope it's enough to get over the Boo. Do it right and the Boo will disappear and you'll get the key.

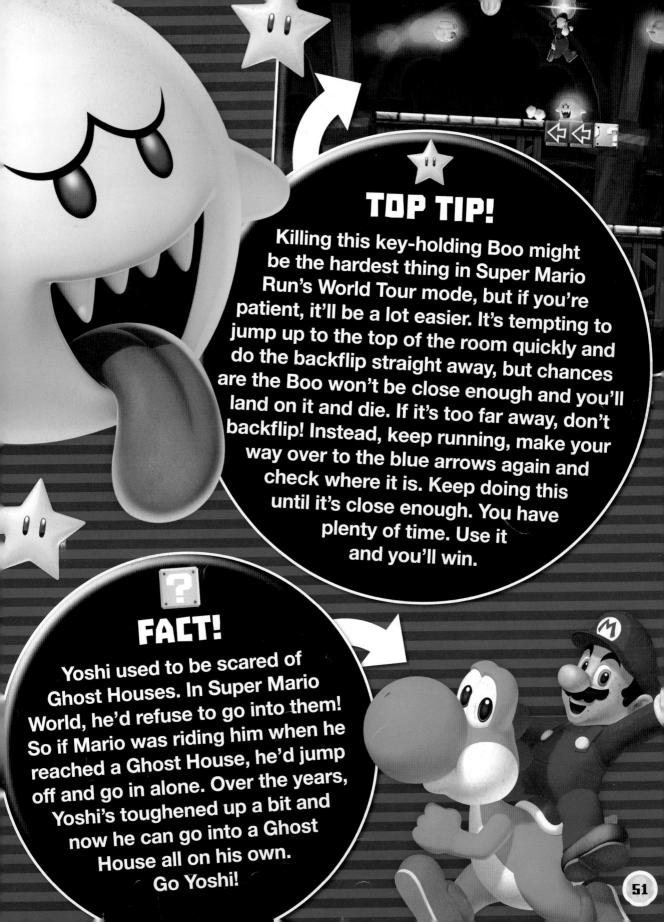

TOP TIP!

Killing this key-holding Boo might be the hardest thing in Super Mario Run's World Tour mode, but if you're patient, it'll be a lot easier. It's tempting to jump up to the top of the room quickly and do the backflip straight away, but chances are the Boo won't be close enough and you'll land on it and die. If it's too far away, don't backflip! Instead, keep running, make your way over to the blue arrows again and check where it is. Keep doing this until it's close enough. You have plenty of time. Use it and you'll win.

FACT!

Yoshi used to be scared of Ghost Houses. In Super Mario World, he'd refuse to go into them! So if Mario was riding him when he reached a Ghost House, he'd jump off and go in alone. Over the years, Yoshi's toughened up a bit and now he can go into a Ghost House all on his own. Go Yoshi!

5-4: RINGS OF FIRE!

Surely the Bowser you're facing this time is the real one? It looks just like him. It's so big and fierce and yellow. It can't be yet another enemy in disguise… It is, though, isn't it? (Sigh.)

FACT!

Bowser might be Mario's sworn enemy but the two have teamed up a few times in the past, mainly in Mario RPG games. Most recently, they joined forces in Mario & Luigi: Bowser's Inside Story. In this game, they work together to fight the evil Fawful (but not before Mario and Luigi are accidentally sucked inside Bowser and have to fight their way out of his insides. Yuck!).

FIRE RINGS

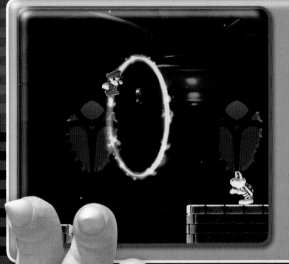

This time Bowser's Castle has a new obstacle – Fire Rings. These can be tricky to get past the first few times but eventually, you get used to them. If you jump too high or too low, you'll hit the fire and take damage. Jump through the middle and you'll be fine. Usually there are coins in the centre which help you aim. Focus on catching these and chances are you'll make it through the ring without even trying.

BOSS LEVEL

Here we go again! The first Bowser we met was a Goomba in disguise, the second pretender was a Koopa Troopa, and this time it's a Buzzy Beetle that wants us to believe it's Bowser. Again, you'll have to beat this one by jumping onto the axe behind him. To make things even trickier, you have a big Fire Ring to deal with, too. If you decide to jump through the ring, you won't have a lot of space to jump over Bowser afterwards. The trick is *not* to go for it straight away. First, stand on the pause block and wait for Bowser to take one or two steps backwards. Time it right and you'll be able to walk through the Fire Ring instead of jumping through it. This will give you plenty of space to jump over Bowser and get to the axe. If you're lucky enough to have found one of those helpful little Mushrooms, you can just plough through this third fake Bowser instead. What's a little damage, after all?

6-1: LAND OF SPIKES

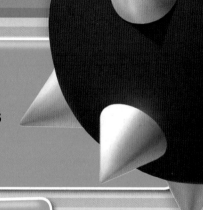

Don't let the name of this level worry you! Spikes are little enemies, not actual spikes. Mind you, they do throw big balls with spikes all over them, so maybe you should worry after all...

ROLLING SPIKED BALLS

Don't think you can relax if you don't see a Spike up ahead. This level also rolls spiked balls at you even when there aren't any Spikes to be seen. When they do appear, Spikes are quite big and you have to clear them completely when you jump over them. Stay on your guard and you should be able to get past them easily enough.

CANNON SCANNIN'

There are a couple of points in this level where you get to fire yourself out of a cannon again. While it's tempting to blast yourself through the coins as quickly as possible, you really have to take your time because there are Spikes chucking balls at you constantly. Try to time it so you fire just as the balls are passing you. This way, they'll have fallen out of the way by the time Mario reaches them.

SPIKES

The game's final world kicks off by introducing you to these odd little fellows. Get near a Spike and it'll pull a big spiked ball out of thin air and throw it towards you. Obviously these will hurt you, so stay well away. If you time it right, you can kill a Spike by jumping on its head. However, every time they pick up a spiked ball, they hold it above their heads first, so if you mistime your jump, you'll be the one getting bopped on the head.

? FACT!

In the 1980s, computer technology was still quite new, so the original Super Mario Bros game was on a cartridge that was only 32KB in size. How small is that? Put it this way – if today's apps were that size, you would be able to download half a million of them on a 16GB phone and still have space left over!

6-2: SWITCH GHOST HOUSE

It's the final Ghost House of the game! This one's all about uncovering secret doors. It can be a bit confusing at first, but follow our steps and you'll breeze through it.

ROOM 1

This level has three rooms you need to escape from. In the first one, you have to stand on the yellow switch on the far right-hand side. This will make a green door appear on the bottom-right of the screen. It can be really easy to miss it because the blue P switch will distract you by revealing loads of coins above. Ignore them and head for the green door below to go to the next room.

ROOM 2

The second room looks easy because you can see the door you need to reach at the top. However, it's swarming with Boos and Stretches so it can be difficult to get up there. Take your time and resist hitting the purple P switch near the door. Although this switch kills all the enemies on the screen at once, it's guarded by a Stretch who keeps appearing above it and hurting you.

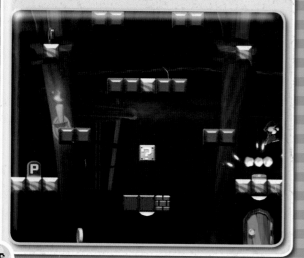

ROOM 3

The final room is the most complicated. You can see the door but you can't reach it without hitting the yellow switch. This fills in the red blocks but makes the door disappear. The trick is to hit this yellow switch and head up to the diagonal jump block on the lower left-hand side of the door. Wait on this block until the yellow switch's power runs out. When this happens, the door will reappear and you'll be in the perfect position to jump over to it.

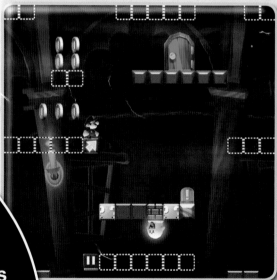

FACT!

Did you know that Super Mario Bros 2 was all just a dream? At the start of the game, Mario finds a door to a mysterious world called Sub-Con. When you beat the game, you see Mario sleeping. It turns out Sub-Con means subconscious, which is a fancy way of saying Mario was dreaming the entire time and the game took place in his brain!

6-3: THROWING IT ALL OVERBOARD

You're nearly at the end of the game, but before you can finally come face-to-face with the real Bowser, Boom Boom has one more airship for you to conquer.

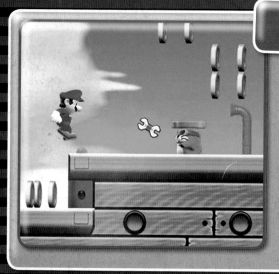

ROCKY WRENCHES

World 6-3 sees the return of the Ninjis from the first airship level, along with a new enemy – Rocky Wrenches. These little moles pop up out of manholes every now and then to throw wrenches at you. Thankfully, when they pop up there's a little pause before they throw, giving you time to get out of the way or jump on their heads. You can even hurdle them before they throw if you're close enough.

FACT!

Can you imagine Mario being a bad guy? Well, he was… but only once. After he rescued his girlfriend in Donkey Kong, Mario put Donkey Kong in a cage. This led to the game Donkey Kong Jr, in which Donkey Kong's son had to rescue his dad from Mario's evil clutches!

⭐ TOP TIP!

Although those pesky little moles usually throw wrenches, some chuck coins instead. If you're close to one, you won't have time to react to whatever it throws, so just assume it's a wrench and jump out of the way. You might miss the coin, but you won't get hit either and that's more important.

BOOM BOOM LEVEL

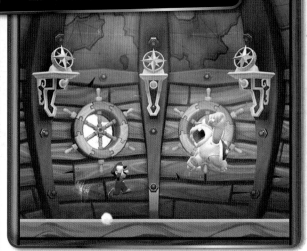

You've got to hand it to Boom Boom, he doesn't know when to quit! Just like in your last two battles with him, you'll have to jump on his head three times to beat him. He's easier to beat than he was in World 4-4 though, because there are no flames getting in your way. Although Boom Boom's new trick is to jump around constantly, you can still jump higher. So you should have no problem landing on his head with a standard jump or a wall-jump.

6-4: BOWSER'S BOB-OMBING RUN

At last you've reached the final level of the game and you can defeat Bowser. Yes, it's really him this time, not an imposter. He's a tricky one if you don't know what you're doing, though!

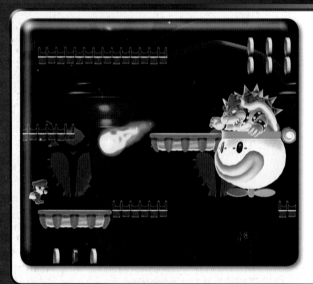

FIRE BREATH

While other boss levels start with normal running and jumping areas, there's none of that here. Right at the start, you have to tackle Bowser. He's got three different methods of attack he deals out randomly. One of these methods is spitting fireballs in your direction. Try to stick to the middle or bottom of the screen because if he breathes fire at you when you're at the top, it's harder to dodge.

SPIKED CANNONBALLS

Bowser also attacks Mario by firing big spiky balls at him. These are a lot like the ones Spike throws at you in World 6-1. When a big cannon comes out of the front of Bowser's ship, he's preparing to attack, so make sure you get up to the highest possible platform. The ball will roll along the platform it lands on and eventually fall to the bottom of the screen. Stick to the top until it's gone, then head back down again.

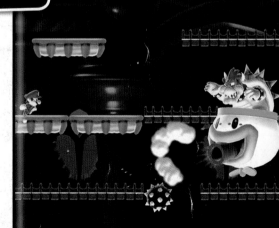

BOB-OMBS

Even the cleverest bad guys can have a flaw in their plan, and the Bob-omb is Bowser's. In other Mario games, these little walking bombs are dangerous because they blow up after a while. In Super Mario Run, however, they don't have time to do this. If you jump on them, or hit them with a mis-hurdle, you'll throw them back in Bowser's direction and hurt him. Send three Bob-ombs Bowser's way and you'll defeat him, completing the World Tour mode!

THE END!

You've done it! You've beaten Bowser and rescued Peach. Or if you've been playing as Peach, you'll have successfully rescued a Toad instead. (If you didn't already know, she's pretty good at taking care of herself!) Whoever you were trying to save, you've done it. Now it's time to go back and do it all over again, this time collecting all those pink, purple and black coins hidden in each level. There's no rest for a Mario hero!

TOAD RALLY MODE

Mastered World Tour mode? Well this next mode will test your skills to the limit. Here, you have to compete against other real-life players to get the most coins. This can be tricky, so follow our tips to increase your chances of winning.

TICKETS

Every time you want to play Toad Rally, it'll cost you one ticket. There are a load of different ways to get Toad Rally tickets, from playing through World Tour mode, to collecting all the coloured coins there, to buying special buildings in Kingdom Builder mode (see page 66). This isn't your usual free-to-play app, though. You can't buy Toad Rally tickets with real money so you'll have to earn them in other ways.

HOW IT WORKS

There are seven possible levels in Toad Rally: grass, desert, sky, underground, fortress, ghost house and airship. Every time you start Toad Rally mode, the game picks five of these and asks you to choose one. The aim is to run through the level collecting as many coins as you can. You get bonus coins for running through checkpoints, collecting Mushrooms, killing enemies and finding pink coins, but you lose coins every time you die so be careful. Unlike World Tour mode, every coin counts so it's worth taking more risks.

STARS

There are Stars hidden in each level of Toad Rally mode. Finding these give you a huge advantage... Not only do they make you invincible (as in other Mario games), but they also begin Coin Rush. Whilst you have a Star, all the nearby coins are pulled towards you like a magnet. Get a Star and run past an area full of coins, and you'll get them all with ease, making your score sky-rocket. Beat your opponent to grabbing a Star and your chances of winning will be much greater.

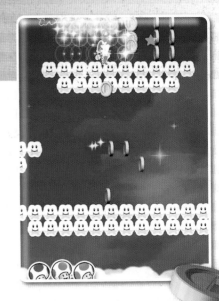

DOING STUNTS

It isn't just collecting coins that builds your score in Toad Rally mode, performing stunts does too. There are loads of moves in the game that count as stunts. Air spins, wall jumps, rolling jumps, vaulting over enemies, and doing combos which hit loads of enemies at once are just some examples of what you can do. Every time you do a stunt, little blue stars will appear under your feet and a Toad will usually appear at the bottom of the screen. When the Rally is over, the number of Toads will be added to the number of coins you've collected for your total score. This means even if you collected slightly fewer coins than your opponent, if you did it with more style, you can still win!

COIN RUSH

When you play Toad Rally mode, there's a blue bar at the top of the screen. Every time you do a stunt the blue bar fills up a little. Fill it completely and you'll enter Coin Rush, which makes you run faster and produces lots of coins. Obviously, the longer you're in Coin Rush the more coins you can get, but be warned because it will run out eventually. The only way to keep it going is to do more stunts so the bar stays full. One final warning: if you die at any time in a level, your blue bar completely empties and you have to start filling it all over again.

TOAD RALLY MODE

QUITTING WHILST YOU'RE BEHIND...

We wouldn't usually recommend quitting a game. However, quitting in Toad Rally mode can sometimes be a useful strategy. If you lose a rally, any Toads you have attracted with your stunts are taken away from your Toad total. So quitting early means you could lose fewer Toads. Also, your Toad Rally ticket will be refunded if you quit so you can use it again for another rally.

LEVELLING UP

Every time you kill an enemy in World Tour or Toad Rally mode, a meter records it. When you have zapped a maximum number of one type of enemy, it levels up. This means you get an extra coin the next time you beat one. Each enemy can level up three times. Why does this matter? Well, let's say you're faced with four Goombas. When you first play the game, you get four coins if you kill them all. After you have beaten enough Goombas and they are fully levelled up, you'll get 16 coins for this. So level up all your enemies and it's easier to win in Toad Rally mode.

PICKING A STAGE

Each of the seven Toad Rally levels gives you different coloured Toads if you win. For example, the grass level has red toads, the underground level has red and blue toads and the desert level has red and yellow ones. Different coloured Toads unlock different buildings in Kingdom Builder mode so you need to get a large number of each colour. Master the airship level, which hosts all five colours of Toad, and you'll never be stuck without the Toad colour you really need.

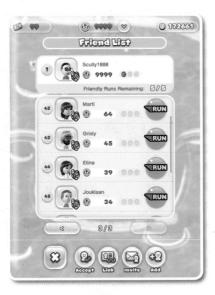

FRIENDLY RUNS

Spent all your Toad Rally tickets? Can't find any more? That's where Friendly Runs come in. Add friends to your game using their unique Player ID (found in the Friends screen) and you'll be able to challenge them in Friendly Runs. These are all just for fun so you can't win or lose any Toads. You can only have five Friendly Runs a day but you'll earn Toad Rally tickets for doing them.

CHARACTERS

Any of the characters you unlock in Super Mario Run can be used in Toad Rally mode, but you need to play to their strengths. Mario and Luigi are probably the safest characters to use because they can take two hits. Toad is fast so, if you're an expert, he can cover more ground and get more coins. However, he can't use Super Mushrooms so, if you haven't had much practice, a single hit will kill him. If you're feeling brave, try playing as Toadette. She can only take one hit, but after a rally ends she'll bump up your score with a few more Toads.

KINGDOM BUILDER MODE

If you've ever wanted to be in charge of your own Mushroom Kingdom, you'll love Kingdom Builder mode! Here you can spend all your hard-earned coins from World Tour and Toad Rally modes on buildings, all sorts of decorations and a few extra special things to make the game more fun.

HOW TO BUILD

Your kingdom is the first thing you see every time you start Super Mario Run. If you want to change how it looks, tap the build icon on the bottom-right of the screen. This lets you move or replace any buildings you already have, as well as buy new ones. Most of the basic items in the shop can be bought with coins. Some of the rare and special items can only be bought with Toads. You'll need to play Toad Rally mode and collect enough Toads before you can buy them.

RAINBOW BRIDGES

You'll quickly see that your kingdom is very small. Not to worry, there's a way around it. As you play the game, you'll unlock Rainbow Bridges which you can then get from the special menu in the shop. These create a rainbow from your kingdom to another area which you can reach by sliding the screen. There are five Rainbow Bridges to unlock. This means you can extend your kingdom until it's made up of six different areas.

BONUS GAME HOUSES

These three special buildings are shaped like mushrooms, and each has a unique mini-game you can play to get extra coins and Toad Rally tickets. Every time you leave a Bonus Game House, it closes down for eight hours to make sure you don't cheat! Visit them regularly though, and you'll always have a ready supply of Toad Rally tickets!

HAMMERS

As you play through World Tour mode, you'll occasionally be given a hammer. These are very useful in Kingdom Builder mode because your kingdom is jam packed with big stone blocks called Whomps. You can't build on top of these and the only way to get rid of them is by smashing them with a hammer. This clears the ground under them and lets you build where they used to stand.

LIMITED ITEMS

Visit the shop as often as you can. Every now and then, Nintendo adds special items… but they don't appear for long! When it first came out, they added a snow globe and a Christmas tree, which soon disappeared. If you see something you like in the Kingdom Builder shop and it has a clock icon next to it, buy it as soon as you can. It won't be there forever and once it's gone, it's gone!

KINGDOM BUILDER MODE

There's a confusing amount of buildings (and other stuff) up for grabs in the Kingdom Builder shop. Some are free, others expensive. Some unlock cool features, others unlock characters. All of them are brilliant fun though! Here's our guide to some of the best ones to look out for...

LUIGI'S HOUSE

Ever wondered where Luigi lives? Well, wonder no more! Buy his house with your coins and Toads, and he'll become available to play!

YOSHI'S HOUSE

So where does Yoshi live, then? In a big egg, of course! Collect enough coins and Toads to buy Yoshi's house and he'll join you in your adventure.

TOADETTE'S HOUSE

Toad's female chum has her own house and it's lovely. Gather enough coins and Toads to buy it and you'll unlock her so she's playable in the game, too.

RED BONUS HOUSE

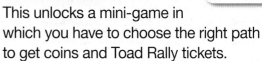

This unlocks a mini-game in which you have to choose the right path to get coins and Toad Rally tickets.

BLUE BONUS HOUSE

Buy this to unlock a mini-game where spinning blocks reveal images if you hit them. Match three in a row to get a prize.

YELLOW BONUS HOUSE

Unlock a room with a pipe spitting out coins and Toad Rally tickets if you buy this house. Keep wall-jumping to collect them, but hit a fireball and it's game over.

QUESTION BLOCKS

There are three of these blocks to buy. Place them in your kingdom and you can tap them periodically to earn Toad Rally tickets and coins, too!

COIN PIPES

Collect all the pink, purple and then black coins in every level in World Tour mode to unlock these three special pipes, which let you play an extra level each!

TOPIARIES

These cleverly cut bushes look like the game's six playable characters. They look great and they aren't too expensive.

8-BIT STATUES

These tributes to the first ever Super Mario Bros game are a great way to celebrate Mario's roots as well as your success!

MODERN STATUES

If you prefer Mario's more up-to-date look, you can get statues of all six current playable characters, too.

BOWSER'S FORTRESS

As the saying goes... keep your friends close and your enemies closer. So with that in mind, Bowser's place might be a good investment for your kingdom...

PEACH'S CAKE

This needs the most Toads to unlock and it's one of the most expensive items, too. You can buy this to put in your kingdom and show everyone you've mastered the game!

MARIO

ABOUT

The main man himself is the hero of the Mushroom Kingdom. He may be small and a bit on the chunky side, but don't let that fool you! When it comes to fighting enemies and rescuing Princess Peach, there's nobody better!

Mario has starred in well over 200 games since he made his debut in Donkey Kong back in 1981. He's one of the most famous characters in gaming history and it doesn't look like he's going to disappear any time soon.

GAMEPLAY

Mario's a good all-rounder, which means he doesn't have any major weaknesses. Not every character in the game can use Super Mushrooms, but Mario's main strength comes from eating them. When he eats one, he grows into Super Mario and can take a hit from an enemy without dying – he just gets smaller instead.

UNLOCKING

You don't have to unlock Mario. When you first start the game, he's already there. It's his name in the title, after all!

LUIGI

ABOUT

Mario's brother may not get as much attention as he does, but that doesn't mean he isn't a brilliant hero too! Sometimes Luigi's a bit cowardly, but when push comes to shove he's always able to swallow his fear and help save the day.

Luigi's been around almost as long as Mario has. He first appeared in Mario Bros in 1983, two years after Mario's debut, and he's been one of the Mario fans' favourite characters ever since. You couldn't have Mario Bros without Luigi!

GAMEPLAY

Like Mario, Luigi can collect Super Mushrooms to make him grow so he can take a hit. However, he can also jump much higher than Mario. This is useful because he can reach platforms and items Mario can't. But it also makes things trickier when you need to do a small jump to avoid getting hit. If you master Luigi he's a better buddy than Mario, but take care!

UNLOCKING

Luigi can be unlocked by playing Toad Rally mode. Once you've got 150 green and 150 purple Toads, you can buy Luigi's House in the Kingdom Builder. Place it in your town and you can play as Luigi.

CHARACTERS

PRINCESS PEACH

ABOUT

You can't have an adventure without a goal and, more often than not, Mario's goal is to rescue Princess Peach. This doesn't mean she's weak though! Even wearing a crown, Peach can run, jump and bounce on baddies' heads just as well as Mario and Luigi can!

She first appeared as Princess Toadstool in Super Mario Bros and she's been around ever since. She has starred in her own DS game – Super Princess Peach – where she got to rescue Mario for a change.

GAMEPLAY

Naturally, Peach has a special power. If you hold your finger on the screen she floats in the air for a few seconds. This means she can do long jumps to reach far away platforms or dodge areas with lots of enemies on the ground. However, she can't use Super Mushrooms so one hit is enough to kill her. You'll need to be careful then!

UNLOCKING

To play as Princess Peach, you have to work your way through World Tour mode. Once you beat Bowser in World 6-4 and watch the scene where Mario rescues her, you can then play as Peach.

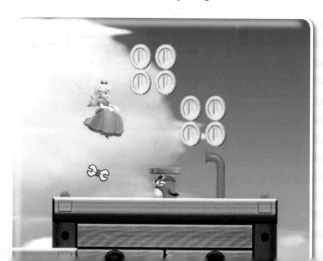

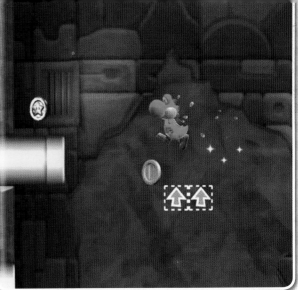

YOSHI

ABOUT

What would a hero be without a trusty steed? We know this is usually a horse, but we'll make an exception for Yoshi.

He popped out of his first egg in Super Mario World back in 1990 and gamers have loved Yoshi ever since. In 2008, a survey in Japan voted him the third best video game character ever, after Cloud from Final Fantasy VII and... Mario, of course!

GAMEPLAY

Yoshi has a signature midair move. Hold your finger on the screen and he'll do his famous flutter-jump. This keeps him in the air a little longer and even lets him travel further upwards. Like Munchers and Piranha Plants, he can also walk on most spiky surfaces without taking damage.

Mario's dinosaur chum has a bottomless stomach and he'll eat almost anything, from enemies to fireballs. He can't eat Super Mushrooms though. So like Peach, one hit and he's gone. Unlike in other Mario games, he can't use his tongue to eat enemies here either.

UNLOCKING

Like Luigi, you can get Yoshi through Toad Rally mode. Buy Yoshi's House with 30 red and 30 yellow Toads in the Kingdom Builder shop to unlock him.

CHARACTERS

TOAD

ABOUT

Size isn't everything, and Toad is proof of this. He may be little, but he's one of the bravest characters in Mushroom Kingdom and he's always got a smile on his face. Toad often acts as Princess Peach's personal guard and he's always keen to help Mario and Luigi.

Like Peach, Toad first appeared in Super Mario Bros in 1985. At the end of each castle level, he delivered his famous line: "Thank you Mario, but our princess is in another castle!"

GAMEPLAY

Toad is the expert's choice because he runs a lot faster than most other characters. In Toad Rally mode, this means you can reach more coins, hit more checkpoints and kill more enemies before time runs out.

However, his speed also makes it easier for you to run into enemies by mistake. Like Peach and Yoshi, he can only take one hit, so only play as Toad if you've mastered the game.

UNLOCKING

You can unlock Toad straight away by linking your game to My Nintendo (see page 76). Set it up and you can get Toad for free from the My Nintendo's Rewards page.

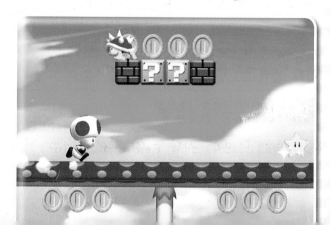

TOADETTE

ABOUT

Toadette is a happy character just like Toad. Rumour has it that she might even be his girlfriend. You can see them holding hands at the ending of Mario Kart Wii. Sweet!

Toadette is the least experienced of the six characters in Super Mario Run, having first appeared in Mario Kart: Double Dash!! on the GameCube in 2003.

GAMEPLAY

Unlike Toad, she runs at normal speed and she plays exactly the same as Mario, except she can only take one hit. When a rally is over, she'll give you a few extra Toads which bump up your score. This means if you've had a close match, you're more likely to win.

UNLOCKING

Toadette will probably be the last character you unlock in the game because getting her takes the most effort. Like Luigi and Yoshi, you get her through Toad Rally mode, but you have to have 1000 Toads in equal numbers of red, blue, green, purple and yellow. Use these to buy her house in Kingdom Builder and set her free.

MY NINTENDO

Super Mario Run links with My Nintendo, which is Nintendo's rewards website. If you sign up as a member of Miitomo, you can collect points to spend on different goodies. Here's how to sign up and what you can do once you have.

HOW TO REGISTER

To sign up to My Nintendo, search online for my.nintendo.com. If you already have a Nintendo account, you can sign up through that, otherwise you'll need to set up a new one. If you're under 13, ask a parent or guardian to create an account for you to use under supervision. Once you sign up, you can tap the My Nintendo icon in Super Mario Run and sign in there to link the game to your account.

COMPLETING MISSIONS

My Nintendo rewards you with points for completing certain missions. Some of them are one-off missions (like beating each world in World Tour mode for the first time) but others can be repeated. For example, play Toad Rally mode on a daily basis and you'll get 10 points each day, then win three rallies in a week to get an extra 50 points. The more points you earn, the more prizes you can buy in the My Nintendo rewards catalogue.

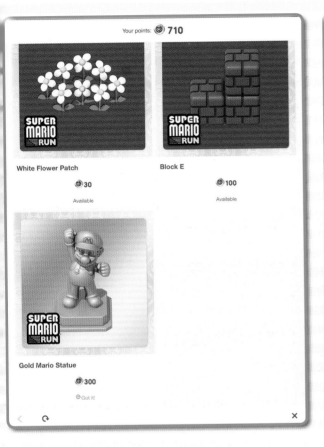

Your points: 710

White Flower Patch
30
Available

Block E
100
Available

Gold Mario Statue
300
Got it!

Hey... What's your favorite food?

SPENDING YOUR POINTS

Head to the Rewards section in My Nintendo and you'll find lots of different goodies to spend your points on. Super Mario Run rewards include decorations for Kingdom Builder mode. If you fancy a massive gold Mario statue in your kingdom, the only way to get it is to spend 300 points in My Nintendo. This is also where you have to go to unlock Toad as a playable character.

MIITOMO

Super Mario Run isn't the only Nintendo app that uses the My Nintendo service. If you have a lot of friends who like using social networks, you might want to give Miitomo a try too. It's a funny app where you're asked questions on lots of different topics and then you get to see how your friends answered them. Just like Super Mario Run, it has missions which let you earn points, and it has its own set of rewards, which include special outfits for your Mii character.

SO YOU THINK YOU KNOW MARIO?

It's time to find out how much you really know about Mario! Check the answers at the bottom of the page to see how you've done... Good luck!

1) What's the name of the Mario Kart game where you have to choose a racing duo?

a) Mario Kart: Double Trouble!!
b) Mario Kart: Double Dash!!
c) Mario Kart: Double Bill!!

2) Which of these isn't a Koopaling?

a) Lemmy
b) Wendy
c) Stiggy

3) Which of these sports has never been in a Mario game?

a) Football
b) Tennis
c) Wrestling

4) What's the name of the only game where Mario was the bad guy?

a) Donkey Kong Jr
b) Wrecking Crew
c) Mario Clash

5) Which of these isn't one of Mario's three princesses?

a) Peach
b) Daisy
c) Rosalina

6) Which of these Super Smash Bros heroes has Mario never battled with?

a) Mega Man
b) Sonic
c) Crash Bandicoot

7) Which EA Sports game did Mario, Luigi and Peach once appear in?

a) FIFA Street 3
b) NBA Street V3
c) NFL Street 3

8) Over the years power-ups have turned Mario into all sorts of animals. Which of these isn't one of them?

a) Penguin
b) Frog
c) Horse

9) What's the name of Magikoopa, the cloaked Koopa Troopa who flies around in some Mario games with a magic wand?

a) Kamen
b) Kamek
c) Kevin

10) What special feature was added to Mario Kart 7 on 3DS?

a) Hang-gliding
b) Racing upside-down
c) Motorbikes

11) What was the first ever game to have both Mario and Sonic in it?

a) Super Smash Bros Brawl
b) Mario & Sonic at the Olympic Games
c) Super Mario Maker

12) Amiibo are small figures that work with some Wii U and 3DS games. Which of these Mario enemies got their own amiibo in 2016?

a) Boo
b) Koopa Troopa
c) Piranha Plant

13) Which Mario character had a special year of games dedicated to them in 2013?

a) Princess Peach
b) Yoshi
c) Luigi

14) There have been four games in the Yoshi's Island series. Which of these wasn't one of them?

a) Yoshi's Island DS
b) Yoshi's New Island
c) Yoshi's Island 2

15) What's the name of the small star that befriends Mario in the Super Mario Galaxy games?

a) Numa
b) Luma
c) Zuma

16) Mario Kart 8 on Wii U had downloadable tracks from other Nintendo games. Which of these didn't have a track in the game?

a) The Legend Of Zelda
b) Animal Crossing
c) Pokémon

17) Why does Mario wear white gloves?

a) It's a tribute to Mickey Mouse
b) In early games it was hard to see his hands
c) Plumbers always wear white gloves

18) Princess Peach was the star of her very own DS game in 2006. What was it called?

a) Super Peach Sisters
b) Super Princess Peach
c) Mario Is Missing

19) Which of these isn't a Toad character in the Mario games?

a) Toadette
b) Toadsworth
c) Lord Toadington

20) What's the name of the inventor who gives Luigi his ghost-hunting vacuum cleaner in Luigi's Mansion?

a) Professer E. Gadd
b) Professor Gad Zooks
c) Professor U. Reka

Answers: 1)b, 2)c, 3)c, 4)a, 5)c, 6)c, 7)b, 8)c, 9)b, 10)a, 11)b, 12)a, 13)c, 14)c, 15)b, 16)c, 17)b, 18)b, 19)c, 20)a

CONGRATULATIONS!

YOU'RE A SUPER MARIO RUN EXPERT!